Cambridge English Readers

···

Level 2

Series editor: Philip Prowse

Logan's Choice

Richard MacAndrew

D1113576

CAMBRIDGE UNIVERSITY PRESS

Cambridge, New York, Melbourne, Madrid, Cape Town, Singapore, São Paulo, Delhi

Cambridge University Press
The Edinburgh Building, Cambridge CB2 8RU, UK

www.cambridge.org
Information on this title: www.cambridge.org/9780521795067

© Cambridge University Press 2000

First published 2000
10th printing 2007

Printed in India by Thomson Press

A catalogue record for this publication is available from the British Library

ISBN 978-0-521-79506-7 paperback
ISBN 978-0-521-68638-9 paperback plus audio CD pack

Illustrations by Debbie Hinks

Contents

People in the story

Inspector Jenny Logan: a police officer in Edinburgh.
Sergeant Grant: an officer helping Inspector Logan.
Alex Maclennan: the owner of Charlotte's Restaurant.
Alice Maclennan: the wife of Alex Maclennan.
Donald Johnstone: Alice Maclennan's brother.
Ian Ross: the manager of Charlotte's Restaurant.
Tam MacDonald: a journalist.
Major Innes: someone who knew Ian Ross when he was a soldier.

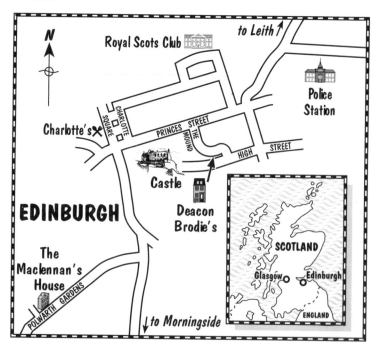

Chapter 1   *Night call*

It was the middle of the night when Jenny Logan's phone woke her. She was tired and answered the phone sleepily.

'Logan.'

'Grant here, madam.'

'It's three o'clock in the morning, Grant. I hope this is important.'

'I'm at the home of Alex Maclennan. He's dead.'

'Give me the address, Grant. I'll be there in twenty-five minutes.'

*   *   *

Jenny Logan was an inspector in the Edinburgh Police. The phone often woke her at night. She got out of bed and dressed quickly in a blue suit. She looked at herself in the mirror and decided that her short brown hair looked all right. By a quarter past three she was driving through the streets of Edinburgh. It was December and there was snow on the ground. Princes Street was empty. She could see Edinburgh Castle high up to her left.

While she drove, Logan thought about Alex Maclennan. The Maclennans were famous in Scotland. Murray Maclennan, Alex's father, had over sixty fish and chip shops in different Scottish towns and cities. Everyone in Scotland knew Maclennan's Fish & Chips and most people ate them.

Murray Maclennan had one son, Alex. Murray did not

want Alex to go into the family business so he sent him to an expensive school in Switzerland. Alex went from there to Bristol University in England, and then to a business school near Boston in the United States. Learning was important for Alex but so was having a good time. The Scottish newspapers were full of stories about his life: he was having dinner with film stars in Cannes; or he was having drinks with sports stars in Monte Carlo; or he was dancing with pop stars at a club in Manhattan. Alex knew how to enjoy himself.

Then six years ago Murray Maclennan died. Alex came back to Edinburgh. He got married and bought a house. Then he sold all the fish and chip shops and, together with an old schoolfriend, Ian Ross, he opened an expensive restaurant in Edinburgh.

Logan drove into Polwarth Gardens and stopped outside Alex Maclennan's house. Logan didn't come to rich areas of the city like this very often. She usually spent more time in the dirtier, poorer areas. Alex Maclennan's house was large and more than one hundred years old.

*   *   *

It was Sergeant Grant who opened the front door. He was fifty-eight and usually he looked young for his age. Tonight he was looking old and tired.

'Hello, madam. Come in,' he said.

'Where's the body, Grant?'

'On the first floor. In the bathroom.'

'The bathroom? OK. Let's go and have a look. What do you know so far?' asked Logan.

They started to climb the stairs.

'Well, madam. Mr Maclennan went to have a bath,

probably at about eleven o'clock. He usually has a bath at about that time,' began Grant.

'I see.'

'Mrs Maclennan was already in bed,' Grant said. 'She says she fell asleep at about ten thirty and didn't hear her husband come up. Anyway, she woke up at one thirty and he wasn't in bed. She thought this was strange so she got up and went to look for him. She couldn't find him but the bathroom door was locked.'

'Did she try and get in?' asked Logan.

'Yes, she tried to break the door open but she couldn't, so she called her brother. He came round, broke open the door and they found Mr Maclennan dead, on the bathroom floor,' finished Grant.

Grant and Logan arrived at the bathroom. The walls were black; the bath, basin and toilet were white; the floor was black and white. Alex Maclennan's body was on the floor. There was a blue towel over his body.

'You say someone locked the door on the inside?' asked Logan.

'That's right, madam,' Grant answered. Grant showed Logan the broken wood.

'Has the doctor seen the body?' asked Logan.

'Yes, madam. He left just before you arrived.'

'So how did he die, then?' asked Logan, looking down at Alex Maclennan's body.

'A broken neck, the doctor says. Looks like the floor was wet, he fell, hit the side of the bath – end of Alex Maclennan.'

Logan looked at the body more closely and then looked round the room. The floor was wet, but not very wet. The

bath was empty. Alex Maclennan's body was dry. The towel was dry too.

'What about the window?' asked Logan.

'I thought about that,' said Grant. 'It's closed but not locked.'

Logan walked across the room and opened the window. She put her head outside and looked down. It was about six metres to the ground – not far.

'Right,' said Logan. 'Get the scientists here. I want them to look everywhere in this room very carefully. They must look at the window and the wall outside, and at the ground outside too.'

'OK, madam,' said Grant.

'Now, where are the family and how are they?'

'Well, there's only Mrs Maclennan and her brother. They're both in the living room,' Grant answered.

Logan went down to the living room. A man and a woman were sitting next to each other on the sofa. The woman was probably in her late twenties but it was difficult to tell because she was crying. She had red hair and was wearing nightclothes.

'Mrs Maclennan, I'm Inspector Logan of the Edinburgh Police,' said Logan. 'I'm very sorry about your husband.'

'Thank you, Inspector,' the woman answered.

The man stood up. He was tall and dark and he looked strong. He was wearing a black jogging suit and he needed a shave.

'Good morning, Inspector. I'm Donald Johnstone, Alice's brother.'

'Hello, Mr Johnstone. I know this is a terrible time for you both, but I'm afraid I have to ask you some questions.'

'Must you?' asked Johnstone. 'Look at my sister. She's crying. Can't you wait?'

'Mr Johnstone, a man has died,' said Logan. 'I am a police officer. I need to find some answers.'

'It's all right, Donald,' said Alice Maclennan. She turned to Logan. 'I understand, Inspector. Please ask your questions.'

'But be quick!' said Johnstone.

'Mrs Maclennan, what time did your husband usually have a bath?' asked Logan.

'Well, he usually went upstairs at about eleven, had a bath and then came to bed,' Alice Maclennan answered.

'When I woke up at about one thirty and he wasn't in bed, I went to look for him.'

Johnstone spoke: 'She called me when she couldn't open the bathroom door. I came as quickly as I could; we broke into the bathroom and found Alex's body. We've told the sergeant this already.'

Logan moved across the room and looked at a photograph of Alice and Alex Maclennan on the day they married. They looked good together.

'Did your husband have any problems, Mrs Maclennan?' asked Logan. 'I mean, business problems.'

'No. I don't think so. Ian Ross took care of the business really. Alex brought his friends to the restaurant so that other people wanted to eat there.'

Logan remembered why people went to Maclennan's

restaurant. It wasn't cheap, but when you went there you almost always saw someone famous.

'So, if I want to find out more about the restaurant, I need to talk to Mr Ross,' Logan said.

'Yes. That's probably best,' Alice Maclennan answered.

'Mrs Maclennan,' asked Logan quietly, 'were you happily married?'

Alice Maclennan looked up quickly at Logan.

Johnstone stood up angrily. 'Now, look here, Inspector. You can't come round here asking questions like that. I must ask you to leave. Please leave now.'

Logan looked hard into Johnstone's eyes, but she spoke to Mrs Maclennan.

'Mrs Maclennan,' she said softly, 'I'm sorry to say this, but it is possible someone killed your husband.'

'You mean . . . ?' began Mrs Maclennan, but she put her hand to her mouth and stopped speaking.

'Yes,' said Logan, turning to her. 'I'm not sure at the moment if it was murder or not.' She turned back to Johnstone. 'So I need answers to difficult questions, Mr Johnstone.'

'Inspector, you can't really think that Alice or I . . . ' started Johnstone.

Logan put up a hand to stop him speaking.

'Mr Johnstone,' she said, 'I don't think anything at the moment. Now, what were you doing when your sister phoned?'

'I was in bed asleep, of course,' said Johnstone in a quiet angry voice.

'With your wife?'

'No, actually. My wife and children are away at the

11

moment. They're staying with my wife's parents until Christmas.'

'So there was nobody there at all except you?' Logan asked quietly.

'That's right.'

Logan looked at Johnstone for some time without speaking. Then she told them both she would like to speak to them again later.

'Was this murder or not?' Logan asked herself. She knew something wasn't right. She knew there was more to find out.

Chapter 2   *Ian Ross*

'Do you really think this is murder?' asked Grant as they sat in Logan's office back at the London Road Police Station.

'I don't know,' answered Logan. 'But I know this: I don't like Mr Johnstone and I don't believe Mrs Maclennan. She hasn't told us everything about her and her husband.'

Grant drank his coffee and Logan looked out of the window. Logan spoke again: 'We won't hear from the scientists until later today. Before then I want you to find out about Mr Johnstone. What's his problem? Why is he so unfriendly?'

'Right, madam,' agreed Grant.

'I'll meet you back here at three o'clock. I'm going to talk to Ian Ross about the restaurant. Perhaps I'll get a free lunch.'

'Police officers never get a free lunch, madam.'

Logan left the police station and drove back to her flat to shower, put on some clean clothes and have something to eat.

Logan lived in Leith, in the north of Edinburgh, by the sea. Many years ago Leith was busy. Lots of boats came in and out every day. These days there were few boats and many of the old buildings were now flats for the young people of Edinburgh. Logan was only twenty-eight but she did not feel young this morning. When she thought about murder, she always felt old.

*   *   *

As Logan drove along Princes Street, there was a loud noise. It came from Edinburgh Castle, Logan's favourite building in the city. The noise was the sound of the one o'clock gun on the castle walls. Every day at one o'clock you can hear the gun. Logan turned right at the end of Princes Street and drove up to Charlotte Square. The restaurant was on the west side of the square. It was called Charlotte's. Logan left her car and went in.

It was busy inside. A waiter walked up to Logan.

'Can I help you, madam?' he asked.

'I'd like to see Ian Ross, please.'

'He doesn't see anyone when the restaurant's open, I'm afraid, madam.'

'I'm Inspector Logan, Edinburgh Police.'

'Ah!' he said. 'Right. Will you follow me, please?'

The man showed Logan into a small office at the back of the restaurant and left her there. A few moments later another man came in. The man was tall with very short blond hair and a small blond moustache. He was in his early thirties and looked strong.

'Inspector. This is terrible news about Alex. Terrible news. He was a wonderful man. A real friend. Now then, how can I help you?'

Logan looked at him.

'Mr Ross?' she asked. Logan took out her ID card and showed it to the man.

'Yes, yes. Sorry. Didn't I say? Ian Ross. Pleased to meet you.' Ross smiled at her.

'Mr Ross, we're not sure how Mr Maclennan died at the moment.'

'Yes. Alice told me. We spoke on the phone this morning,' said Ross.

'I'm just asking a few questions so I can find out a little more about him,' said Logan.

'Of course. Please ask anything you like.'

'Well, when did you first meet Mr Maclennan?' asked Logan.

'Oh years ago,' answered Ross. 'We went to school together when we were young. Then he went to Switzerland and travelled all over the world.'

'And what about you?' she asked.

'I stayed here until I was sixteen. Then I joined the army, became a soldier, and travelled the world too,' said Ross.

'Did you see each other often?' asked Logan.

'No. Not often,' he said. 'But if we were both in Edinburgh at the same time we always got together.'

'When did you start this place?'

'About five years ago,' said Ross. 'I left the army and came back here. I didn't have a job. Alex was back from the States. We spent a lot of time together and decided to start Charlotte's. He had the money and the famous friends. I did the work!' Ross laughed, but Logan saw that his eyes were not smiling.

'Is the restaurant making money?' asked Logan.

'Yes. As you can see, we're very busy. We're always very busy. The restaurant is doing very well.'

'You must earn a lot then. Did you each take half of the money or . . . ?'

'No. If you must know, Alex paid me. I'm the manager. But I don't see how this is important.'

'I don't know if it is important, Mr Ross. Tell me, were you here last night?'

'Yes, Inspector. Until about eleven. Then I went home. I usually stay later but yesterday I was tired. I went home and went to bed early.'

'Do you live by yourself, Mr Ross?'

'Yes.'

'So,' Logan thought to herself, 'no-one knows if you were at home or not.' She spoke again.

'How well do you know Alice Maclennan?'

'Now wait a minute, Inspector. If you think Alice and I . . . ' He stopped.

Logan looked at Ross.

'I don't think anything, Mr Ross. Like I said, I just ask questions.'

Chapter 3   *Help from friends*

When Logan got back to the London Road Police Station, Grant was waiting for her with some interesting news.

'Donald Johnstone is a man with a lot of problems and not much money,' Grant began.

'Really?' said Logan. 'Tell me more.'

'Well, four years ago he borrowed some money from the bank. He started a business buying and selling used cars.'

'I thought used-car salesmen always made money,' said Logan, smiling.

'Not at the moment,' said Grant. 'The price of new cars has come down over the last two years. And because of that the price of used cars has come down too. So business has been difficult for Mr Johnstone. And . . . he keeps his cars at a place in the West End, not far from Princes Street.'

'That's an expensive place to have a business,' Logan said.

'Very expensive,' agreed Grant.

Most garages and car salesmen are outside the city, not right in the centre.

'So how bad is the problem?' asked Logan.

'Very bad,' said Grant. 'He's borrowed £200,000 from the bank over the past four years and now they want the money back.'

'Can he pay it back?'

'No,' answered Grant. 'But he's got a nice house quite

near his sister. If he can't find the money by the end of the year, the bank is going to take his house.'

'His wife won't be very happy,' said Logan.

'No,' Grant agreed.

'Is he hoping his sister will help him?'

'Well, she'll have a lot of money now, won't she?' said Grant.

'Yes,' said Logan. 'She will.'

Logan looked at Grant. He had thick black hair and a large black moustache. He was wearing an old blue jacket and old grey trousers. He did not really look like a policeman, but he was very good at getting information.

'Well done, Grant!' She smiled at him. 'And where did you find out all that?'

'Oh, you know, here and there,' said Grant. 'Of course it helps that my cousin and Johnstone's wife are good friends.'

Logan laughed.

At that moment the phone rang. Grant answered it. For most of the conversation he just listened. Then he thanked the person and put the phone down. He turned to Logan.

'That was Dr Forbes. The scientists have finished. Maclennan died some time between eleven thirty and twelve thirty of a broken neck – they can't say if it was murder.'

'We knew that,' said Logan. 'Anything else?'

'They found a very small piece of black material on the window lock, and another very small piece on the wall outside the bathroom. They think the material probably came from someone's clothes.'

They looked at each other.

'It is murder, isn't it?' said Grant.

'Well, I don't think someone climbed into the bathroom to have a shower, do you?' said Logan.

*　　*　　*

Logan sent Grant round to Polwarth Gardens. She wanted to be sure that the black material did not come from Alex or Alice Maclennan's clothes. She told Grant to take any black or dark blue clothes and ask the scientists to have a look at them.

Soon after Grant left, Logan decided to find out if the Maclennans really were happily married. She could make a phone call but it was more interesting to talk to people face to face. She put on her coat and went out onto London Road. She walked up Leith Street and turned into Princes Street. Princes Street is unusual for the main street of a large city. There are shops on only one side of the street. The Princes Street Gardens are on the other side. In the summer the gardens are full of people sitting in the sun. Today there was snow on the ground and there were only a few people in the gardens. They were hurrying to get in from the cold.

Logan enjoyed her walk in the cold air. She walked up The Mound, looking at the beautiful tall buildings. This side of Princes Street was called the Old Town. The other side, already more than two hundred years old, was called the New Town. Logan soon turned left and walked into the offices of the *Scottish Daily News*. She went up to the newsroom on the first floor. It was full of journalists. A short man with red hair and glasses looked up from his work.

'Well, Jenny Logan,' said the man. 'How nice to see you! You're just in time to buy me a Christmas drink.'

'OK, Tam,' said Logan. 'But you'll have to work for it. I want some information from you.'

'Oh, Inspector, you're a hard woman. You think I'll tell you everything you want just because I like you so much.'

'Come on, Tam, let's go,' laughed Logan.

A few minutes later Logan and Tam were sitting in Deacon Brodie's, a famous old pub on the High Street.

'What do you know about the Maclennans, Tam?' asked Logan.

'Not much more than you probably,' said Tam. 'Alex came back from America, married a beautiful red-headed actress and started a restaurant. He's got lots of money from his father, lots of famous friends, and a fine house in a nice area of the city. Well, he had all these things until last night.'

'Yes. I know all that. That's what I read in the papers. But what else do you know? What do you know that you don't put in the paper?'

Tam finished his drink and looked at the empty glass.

'I get thirsty when I talk a lot,' he said.

Logan smiled and went up to the bar. While she was waiting for their drinks, she turned round and looked at Tam. He was looking out of the window at the shoppers in the High Street. It was unusual for a journalist and a police officer to be friends. But Jenny Logan liked Tam a lot and she knew that he liked her.

When she came back to their table, Tam spoke: 'Everyone thought that the Maclennans had a wonderful life. The restaurant is always busy. Alex's friends were always there. Alice always had a smile on her face. But . . . '

'But . . . ?'

'For the last eighteen months or so something was wrong,' said Tam. 'They weren't happy.'

'How do you know?' asked Logan.

'Little things,' said Tam. 'Somebody heard them shouting at each other one night. A few weeks later she went on holiday without him. She stopped going to the restaurant so often. In the old days they were very close. But for the last year or two it was unusual to see them together.'

'Do you think she had a lover? Or did he?' asked Logan.

'Ah! Now that's the question.'

'Come on, Tam! What's the answer?' laughed Logan. 'And it doesn't cost another drink.'

Tam laughed and then started talking again.

'Well, the answer is that if anyone had a lover, she did. Alex didn't have enough time to see anyone else. He was almost always at the restaurant or at home. But we think Alice was probably seeing someone else. Nobody is sure. And nobody knows who the other man is, or was.'

'Did you try and find out?' asked Logan.

'Of course. I mean, we are journalists, you know!'

Logan smiled. Tam spoke again.

'One of our men followed her a few times when he wasn't busy. But he didn't find anything. The strange thing was he lost her twice. Both times it was a Thursday evening.'

'So you never found out if there was another man?' asked Logan.

'No,' said Tam. 'We wanted to find out more, but we couldn't spend all our time following her. There were other more important stories.'

'Well, thanks, Tam. You've given me some good information. It's very kind of you.'

Tam put his hand on Jenny Logan's, looked into her eyes and gave her a big smile.

'I'm a very kind man, you know, Jenny Logan.' Then his voice changed and he said quickly, 'So tell me, was it murder? And if so, who did it?'

Logan laughed. Tam's hand felt warm and nice, but she took hers away. Slowly.

'I don't know who did it, Tam,' she said. 'But it was murder. And you can put that in the paper, if you want.'

'Well, well, well. So it *was* murder then,' said Tam. 'Thanks, Jenny.'

'Yes,' said Logan. 'And you are such a kind man that when I know who did it, I'll tell you first.'

Tam smiled at her.

Logan left Tam in Deacon Brodie's and decided to go and meet Grant at Polwarth Gardens. She took her phone out of her bag and called Grant. It was time to find out what the Maclennans' marriage was really like.

Chapter 4   *Alice Maclennan*

For the second time that day Grant opened the door when Logan arrived at the Maclennans' house in Polwarth Gardens. He followed her through the house to the living room.

'Johnstone's gone home and will be back tomorrow,' said Grant. 'I didn't tell him you were coming.'

'Good. Have you found any black clothes?' asked Logan.

'A black pullover and some black trousers,' answered Grant. 'They were Alex Maclennan's. Mrs Maclennan doesn't have any dark clothes at all.'

'Well, that's interesting,' said Logan. 'Of course, she

could easily wear her husband's clothes. Get those clothes to the scientists as soon as possible. We really need to know who was climbing in or out of . . .' She stopped speaking as they arrived at the living room door.

Alice Maclennan was standing behind a beautiful antique desk and studying some papers. She looked up when Logan and Grant came into the room.

'Inspector Logan,' she said. 'What can I do for you?'

'I'm sorry, but I'm afraid I have some more questions,' said Logan.

'That's all right, Inspector. Shall we sit down?'

Alice Maclennan walked across the room and sat down on the large green sofa. She was wearing light grey trousers and a white blouse. Logan sat in an armchair close to the sofa. Grant stood by the door.

'As Sergeant Grant found out, I have no dark clothes,' said Alice Maclennan. 'People usually wear black after someone has died. But Alex will have to be happy with grey.' She smiled sadly.

'I'm sure he won't mind,' said Logan softly.

Alice Maclennan looked up. 'Anyway, you must ask me your questions.'

Logan looked round the room at the beautiful antique furniture and the old pictures on the walls.

'What happens to all this now?' asked Logan. 'Who gets the house and your husband's money? What happens to the restaurant?'

'Well, that's easy,' said Alice Maclennan. 'He left everything to me. I get the house and the money – everything except the restaurant.'

'Not the restaurant?' asked Logan.

'No, the restaurant is different. The restaurant was always Alex's and Ian's. Ian didn't have any money when they started so Alex paid him to be the manager. But Alex always said that the restaurant was theirs. Fifty-fifty. So now Alex is dead, I will get half of it and the other fifty per cent will go to Ian.'

'Did Mr Ross know about this?' asked Logan.

'Of course, Inspector,' answered Alice Maclennan. 'He and Alex talked about it when they started the restaurant.'

'So they were very good friends?' asked Logan.

'That's right.'

Logan's dark brown eyes studied Alice Maclennan's face carefully.

'They were good friends when they started the restaurant. I know that,' said Logan. 'But did they stay good friends? I mean, I've heard that Mr Ross did all the work and Alex didn't do very much. It was Alex who was famous. Everyone came to see Alex's friends. How did Mr Ross feel about that?'

Alice Maclennan looked away from Logan. Her fingers started playing with a ring on her finger. She looked back at Logan and met her eyes.

'I really don't know, Inspector,' she said. 'You'll have to ask him. I don't often go to the restaurant these days. I don't see Ian very often.'

Logan was quiet for a moment.

'You didn't answer my question this morning,' she said.

'What question was that?' Alice asked quickly – almost too quickly.

'Were you and your husband happily married?'

'Of course we were,' said Alice.

'Mrs Maclennan,' said Logan. 'I don't believe that is true. And you know it isn't true.'

Logan looked into Alice Maclennan's eyes.

'Please, Mrs Maclennan. I'm looking for the person who murdered your husband. I know this is a very difficult time for you. I don't want to make it more difficult, but you must help me.'

Alice Maclennan started to cry.

'No, we weren't happily married,' she said. 'When we first got married we were. We were so, so happy. We were in love and everything was wonderful for a few years. Then Alex and Ian started the restaurant. It took more and more of Alex's time. It was stupid really. He didn't do any of the hard work, but he spent more and more time at the restaurant. Sometimes we didn't see each other for days. I became bored . . . and angry.'

'Were you angry with each other just before he died?' asked Logan.

'No. Things were beginning to change. So no, we weren't angry with each other.' Alice Maclennan looked out of the window. She thought carefully as she spoke. 'We were starting to be happy again. About six months ago we had a long talk about our marriage. Alex said he was sorry I was so angry. He said he wanted to spend more time with me. He wanted to try and make me happy again.'

'Mrs Maclennan, when your husband was spending a lot of time at the restaurant, did you have a lover?' asked Logan.

Alice Maclennan looked at the Inspector. This time she did not look away.

'No,' she said.

Logan looked at her, but said nothing.

'No, Inspector, I did not,' she said.

Logan stood up.

'Well, thank you for your time, Mrs Maclennan,' she said. 'I hope I don't need to ask you anything else, but if I do, I know where to find you.'

*   *   *

'What do you think, Grant?' asked Logan. They stood outside the house in Polwarth Gardens.

'What do you mean, madam?' asked Grant.

'Did she have a lover or didn't she? You were watching her. Do you believe her?'

'You still don't?'

'I'm not sure,' answered Logan. 'I believe what she said about her marriage. But I think she had a lover . . . or maybe still has a lover.'

'And the lover could be the murderer?' asked Grant.

'That is very possible, Grant. But if there is a lover, nobody knows who it is at the moment. Alice Maclennan certainly isn't going to tell us. So let's think of something else to do.'

Logan told Grant about her visit to the restaurant and what she had found out from Tam. She asked Grant to send Alex Maclennan's clothes to the scientists and then go to the restaurant. She wanted more information about Ian Ross from the people who worked there. She wanted to know how Ross felt about Alex Maclennan.

Logan started thinking about Donald Johnstone. He needed lots of money and he needed it quickly. His brother-in-law was dead and his sister was now very rich. Was he just lucky or was he too lucky? She decided she had some questions for him.

Chapter 5 *Two angry men*

Logan did not know where to find Donald Johnstone – at home or at work. She called his home number and he answered the phone. She put the phone down without speaking. Five minutes later she arrived at his house in Morningside.

Johnstone opened the door. He was wearing a dark grey suit and a black tie.

'Yes, Inspector?' he said.

'Mr Johnstone, I'd very much like to ask you one or two more questions,' said Logan.

'Inspector,' he said, 'I'm very busy. I'm afraid I have no time at all.'

'You've got a choice, Mr Johnstone. We can talk now and it will take about ten minutes. Or, I can take you to the police station and ask you some questions there. Perhaps you'll be home again by tomorrow morning. I believe the beds at the police station are rather uncomfortable too.'

'That's not much of a choice!' said Johnstone. 'Come in, and let's be quick.'

Logan went into the house and followed Johnstone into the living room. Johnstone did not ask Logan to sit down. He stood behind an armchair and turned to her.

'Well?' he asked.

'How's your business doing, Mr Johnstone?'

'Fine,' said Johnstone. He put his hands on the back of the chair in front of him.

'I understand that actually business is not so good just now.'

'It's just a small problem,' said Johnstone. 'And it's a problem which will soon go away. People always start buying cars in the New Year and I'll start earning money again.'

'I understand that your bank probably won't wait until the New Year.'

'Well, you must know something that I don't know. When I last spoke to my bank manager, he was very happy to wait until the end of January.'

'Really?' Logan looked round the room. 'You have a very nice house, Mr Johnstone. I'm sure you don't want the bank to take it away from you because you can't pay them back.'

'That's not going to happen,' said Johnstone angrily. His face was going red.

'Why not? Because your brother-in-law is dead and so your sister now has enough money to help you,' said Logan quietly.

'What are you saying, Inspector? That I wanted Alex dead? That I had something to do with it?'

Johnstone's face was now dark red with anger.

'Get out!' he shouted. 'Get out of my house and don't come back.'

Logan turned and walked to the front door. Johnstone had big problems and he was an angry man. Was he angry because his business was doing badly? Or was he angry because of something else? Logan did not know. The important question was: did he need money badly enough to kill his brother-in-law?

Outside, she got into her car and looked at her watch. It was now six o'clock and snow was falling again. She sat in the car and thought more about Johnstone. He was wearing a dark suit this evening. But what did he have on this morning? She tried to remember but couldn't.

Logan decided to go back to the police station. She hoped that Grant was still there. While she drove, she thought about Ian Ross. It was interesting that he now had fifty per cent of the restaurant. Logan knew people who killed for fifty pounds. Fifty per cent of Charlotte's was much more than fifty pounds.

When she drove into the car park at the London Road Police Station, she saw Grant's car. Good. He was still there. She ran up the stairs and found him in his office. When she came into the room, he smiled.

'You know, madam, I think Ross really hated Maclennan.'

'So you had an interesting visit,' said Logan, smiling. She sat down opposite Grant.

'Yes,' said Grant. 'Very interesting. Ross was out, so the people at the restaurant were happy to talk to me.'

'Good. So? What did they say?'

'Well, the most interesting person was one of the waitresses, a woman called Isabel Ferguson. She's been at Charlotte's right from the start.'

Grant stopped and drank some coffee. 'She said it was a great place to work at first. Ross and Maclennan talked to all the people who came to eat there. Alice was there most of the time. The three of them told funny stories about each other. Everyone was always laughing. She said it was a great place to be, a great place to work.'

'But . . .' said Logan.

'But the last year and a half have been terrible. Alice Maclennan doesn't come to the restaurant any more. Alex Maclennan wasn't as much fun as before. And Ross almost never comes out of the kitchen.'

'Does she know why?' asked Logan.

'Well, the problem was that Ross and Maclennan stopped being friends. She thinks it was because of money. Maclennan was earning a lot of money from the restaurant. Everyone knew that. But he was still paying Ross the same as when they started.'

'And Ross didn't like it,' said Logan.

'Isabel thinks he didn't like it at all.'

'Did he talk to anyone about it?' asked Logan.

'No. She and Ross are good friends, but he never said

anything to her. One night after the restaurant closed, she heard Ross and Maclennan shouting at each other in the office. Later she asked Ross what the problem was and he told her it wasn't important.'

Grant stopped speaking. Logan sat quietly. Then she looked at Grant.

'We must have a closer look at Mr Ross, I think,' she said.

'Yes, madam,' said Grant.

'He was in the army, wasn't he? I want to talk to someone about his time in the army.' She looked at her watch. It was seven thirty. 'But it will be much too late now. Can you find me a number to call in the morning? Then go home and I'll see you tomorrow. We can't do anything else today.'

'OK, madam.'

Logan got her bag and coat, then left the office. Outside it was dark. On her way home she stopped at a supermarket to buy some food. She drove home and left her car in the street outside her house.

When she got inside, she made a sandwich, opened a bottle of Pepsi and sat down. She started thinking about Alex Maclennan's murder again. Did Alice Maclennan have a lover? Who? Why was Donald Johnstone so angry? How did he feel about Alex? Was he at home before his sister phoned? Did the bank want to take away his house? Who wanted Alex dead?

Logan's last thought was about Ian Ross. What did he do in the army? She needed to find out more in the morning.

Chapter 6 *Blood on their hands*

Grant called Logan at home early the next morning.

'I've found someone who knows Ian Ross,' he said. 'He's called Major James Innes. He said he'll meet you at the Royal Scots Club at eleven o'clock this morning. Ask for him at the main office and they will tell you where to find him.'

'Thanks, Grant.'

At a quarter to eleven Logan was walking down Queen Street in the New Town. The weather had become very cold. Logan was wearing a thick coat, a scarf and a hat. Her nose was red with the cold. She kept her hands in her pockets and her head down against the wind.

The Royal Scots Club was on the other side of the Queen Street Gardens in Abercromby Place. The club was a meeting place for a lot of people, not just old soldiers. There was a restaurant and a bar, meeting rooms and also a number of bedrooms where people could stay. It was a sort of hotel as well as a club.

Major Innes was waiting for Logan in a quiet room near the main office. He was sitting in an armchair in front of a warm fire. He was about sixty years old with short white hair and a white moustache. He was wearing a dark blue jacket and an army tie.

'Good morning, Inspector,' he said. 'Your sergeant told me you wanted some information about Ian Ross.'

'Yes, Major. How well did you know Ross?'

'Very well. He was one of my men for a number of years.'

'Well, I'd like to know anything you can tell me about him,' said Logan.

'He was a good soldier, a very good soldier,' said Major Innes. 'He always did what I asked. He was intelligent and he was strong.'

'Were you together for a long time?' asked Logan.

'About four or five years.'

'Where?'

'I'm sorry, Inspector,' said Major Innes. 'I can't give you that sort of information. You see, we were in the SAS. We are not allowed to talk about where we have been and what we were doing.'

Logan sat back in her armchair and looked at the major. The SAS were some of the best soldiers in the British

Army. They often worked in very dangerous places, sometimes inside countries that were not at all friendly to Britain. The SAS knew the meaning of danger. They were hard men.

'I didn't know Ross was in the SAS,' said Logan quietly.

The fire was very warm but Logan felt cold. She thought for a moment. Then she spoke: 'Major, I must tell you why I'm here. I'm looking for the person who killed Alex Maclennan. You've probably read about his murder in the papers.'

'Yes, Inspector,' said the Major.

'Well, Ian Ross and Alex Maclennan were good friends at one time. They had a restaurant business together.'

'I see. And do you think Ross murdered Maclennan?' asked the major.

'Major, did Ian Ross kill anyone when he was in the army?' asked Logan, not answering the major's question.

'Yes, Inspector, he did. A number of people. But you must remember that he was a soldier. It was his job. Soldiers only kill when they have to. They do not kill their friends.'

'No,' thought Logan. 'Soldiers don't kill their friends.' But were Ian Ross and Alex Maclennan friends or not?'

'Thank you very much, Major. I'm sorry I've taken so much of your time.' She stood up to go.

'That's all right, Inspector. I hope you find the right person. Ian Ross was a very good soldier and he killed people when he had to; but that doesn't mean he is a murderer.'

*　　*　　*

Logan left the Royal Scots Club. She walked back to Queen Street where she stopped a taxi. It took her back to

London Road. She got a cup of coffee and sat in her office. She looked out of the window. In the garden on the other side of the street some children were playing in the snow. They were laughing and shouting and building a snowman.

Logan's phone rang. She answered it.

'Logan,' she said.

'This is your favourite newspaper journalist speaking.' It was Tam's voice.

Logan smiled to herself. 'Hi, Tam!' she said. 'If you're phoning about the Maclennan murder, I'm afraid I haven't got anything for you.'

'That's OK, Jenny,' said Tam, 'because I could have something for you.'

Logan pulled her notebook out of her bag.

'What is it, Tam?'

'How much do you know about Donald Johnstone?'

'Well, we know all about his business and his problems with the bank,' said Logan.

'Ah!' said Tam. 'Then you don't know that he nearly killed a man three years ago.'

'What!' Logan almost shouted into the phone. 'How do you know that?'

'Interesting, isn't it?' said Tam. 'Another journalist here at the *News* is working on the Maclennan murder. He was talking to someone who knows Johnstone and this story came out.'

'Go on,' said Logan.

'Well, I don't know if this is true, but anyway . . . you know Johnstone buys and sells used cars.'

'Yes,' said Logan.

'Well, three years ago a man called Neil Erskine came to Johnstone. Erskine said he had three BMWs to sell. He told Johnstone that he had an expensive taxi company for rich business people. He was buying some new cars for the company and he wanted to sell the old ones.'

Logan could see what was coming.

'How much of the story was true?' she asked.

'You *are* good at your job, Jenny,' he laughed. 'Well, he wanted to sell three BMWs, but nothing else was true.'

'But Johnstone believed him?' said Logan.

'Yes. He bought the BMWs, and then about a week later the police came round and took all three of them away. They weren't Neil Erskine's at all. Two of them were from the south of England and one was from Liverpool.'

'And where was Neil Erskine?' asked Logan. But she knew the answer.

'Gone,' said Tam.

'So what happened?' asked Logan.

'Well, Neil Erskine wasn't his real name. His real name is Neil Gordon and he's from Glasgow. But Johnstone didn't know that. Anyway, about a year later Johnstone was over in Glasgow doing some business. He was in a pub and . . .'

'He saw Neil Gordon,' said Logan.

'Right again,' said Tam. 'Well, Johnstone followed him home. Later that week he went back with three of his friends. Neil Gordon spent the next three months in hospital. And now, three years later, he still can't walk very well.'

'He didn't tell the police about Johnstone.'

'No, he didn't. If the police found out about the cars . . .' Tam stopped speaking.

'I see what you mean,' said Logan.

She said nothing as she thought about Johnstone. She knew that he got angry very quickly. But she didn't know that he could do something like this.

'Are you still there?' asked Tam.

'Oh! Sorry, Tam,' she said. 'Look, thanks very much. What you've told me is a real help. You journalists have some very interesting friends.'

Tam laughed. 'I'll speak to you later,' he said.

'Bye,' said Logan and put the phone down. Tam's news about Johnstone was interesting, but what could she do with it? It didn't mean Johnstone was a murderer. But now Logan was sure he could kill, if he wanted to.

She looked out of the window. The children's snowman was finished and snowballs were flying through the air.

She let different ideas run through her head. After a time one idea stayed there and she thought about it very carefully.

Some time later Logan heard the one o'clock gun and Sergeant Grant put his head round the door.

'Come in, Grant,' she said. 'Tell me what you think of my idea.'

It took Logan about twenty minutes to tell Grant what she wanted to do. Then they got everything ready. After that Logan phoned Alice Maclennan and told her that she would like to come round and see her again.

She stood up and turned to Grant.

'Get three officers and I'll see you in about half an hour,' she said.

Chapter 7   *Catching a murderer*

At five thirty that evening Logan followed Alice Maclennan into her living room. As they sat down, Alice Maclennan spoke.

'You said on the phone, Inspector, that you needed my help. I don't see how I can help you. I've already told you everything I know.'

'I know,' said Logan, 'but I'd like you to do something for me, and my hope is that we can then catch the person who murdered your husband.'

'What do you mean?' asked Alice Maclennan.

Logan looked into Alice's eyes.

'Mrs Maclennan,' asked Logan softly, 'have you thought about who the murderer could be?'

'I'm hoping that it's someone who broke into the house looking for money,' she said quietly, 'but I think it probably isn't.'

Logan said nothing. Alice Maclennan looked at Logan and then down at her hands.

'I think it's probably someone I know,' said Alice Maclennan, 'maybe someone I'm close to. And that's a terrible thought.'

'I know. It must be very difficult for you,' said Logan. 'Sadly, it almost certainly is someone close to you or your husband.'

Alice Maclennan stood up and walked across the room to the window. Then she turned round and looked at Logan.

'Well, who do you think it is and what do you want me to do?' she asked.

'As far as I can see, it's good news for two people that your husband is dead – Ian Ross and your brother. Ross hated Alex. Your brother needs money badly and you will now be very rich.'

Alice Maclennan sat down again.

'That's true,' she said very quietly.

'What I want you to do,' said Logan, 'is phone both Ross and your brother. Tell them that Mr Fraser, who lives in Harden Place just behind your house, has called the police. He saw someone climbing into your bathroom the night your husband was murdered. Tell Ross and your brother the police artist is going to Harden Place tomorrow morning to draw a picture of the person Mr Fraser saw.'

'And what do you think will happen?' asked Alice Maclennan.

'The murderer will want to talk to Mr Fraser,' answered Logan, 'and we will be there waiting.'

Alice Maclennan sat quietly, thinking.

'I need to think what to say,' she said.

Logan sat quietly. Alice Maclennan looked at her and gave a small smile. 'Did you know that I was an actress before I met Alex?' she said.

'Yes, I knew that,' said Logan.

Alice Maclennan turned and picked up the phone.

*   *   *

Harden Place was a small street near Polwarth Gardens. Number eight was on the left-hand side of the street. It had a small front garden and a red front door.

The ground floor of the house was quite small. At the back of the house was a long living room with double doors which opened into the back garden. There were trees in the back garden and a wall on each side.

In the living room a man was sitting in an armchair in front of the fire. He was wearing old grey trousers and an old blue jacket and he had a large black moustache. He was smoking a cigarette and reading the newspaper. It was eleven o'clock in the evening and dark outside.

There were three other doors from the living room. One led into the hall; a second led into a small room at the front of the house; the third led into the dining room, also at the back of the house, between the living room and the kitchen.

In the front room the lights were off. The door was open a few centimetres. Three police officers were sitting behind

41

the door. Inspector Logan was standing just inside the door. She could see into the living room. The man in the armchair was Sergeant Grant.

Sometimes he looked up at the clock, and then he went back to reading his paper. Logan watched the smoke from his cigarette going up in a line. After a few minutes the smoke stopped going up in a line. It moved slowly around.

The house was quiet. Logan felt cold air coming in. Grant put the newspaper down on the floor next to his chair. As he did this, the door behind him, which led to the dining room, opened very quietly.

A tall man, dressed from head to foot in black, came through the door into the room. He had a sort of black hat over his head and face, too. Only his eyes showed. There was a knife in his hand. Logan could see that Grant was ready.

Grant stood up quickly and turned round. The man in black moved to his left. Grant moved too. He moved away, watching the man with the knife carefully. Logan waited.

The man in black spoke softly. 'You think you saw me, do you?' he said. 'You think you can tell the police who I am. Well, I'm sorry but I've got no choice, I can't let you do that.'

The man in black ran quickly over to Grant. Logan decided she could wait no longer. 'Now!' she shouted.

She ran into the living room. The police officers followed her, but they were all too late. The man in black had his arm around Grant's chest. The knife was at Grant's throat, and a little blood was running down Grant's neck to his shirt.

42

'Don't come near me or I'll kill him,' said the man in black.

'Drop the knife. You can't get away,' said Logan quietly.

Nobody moved.

'Get away from the door or Fraser dies,' shouted the man in black. 'Get away from the door.'

Again nobody moved.

Then Logan spoke: 'It's over Ross. That is Sergeant Grant, not Mr Fraser. Let him go.'

The room was quiet. The knife moved a few centimetres away from Grant's throat. Grant was ready. His elbow moved back very hard and very quickly into the stomach of the man behind him. The man dropped his knife. His hands flew to his stomach. He fell to the floor. Quickly Grant picked up the knife.

Logan walked across the room and pulled off the black hat. Ross's face was dark, his eyes black and angry.

'How did you know it was me? How did you know I killed Alex?' he asked.

'Why did you do it?' asked Logan.

'He was so pleased with himself. He loved everyone thinking he was rich and funny. He loved telling me how much money he earned from the restaurant. I asked him to pay me more, but he said no. He laughed at me when he said it.'

'Did you know you got fifty per cent of the restaurant if he died?' asked Logan.

'That's what he told me,' answered Ross. 'Sometimes I believed it, sometimes I didn't. It wasn't important anyway. He had everything: money, the restaurant, a beautiful wife. I hated him. I hated him so much I wanted him to die.'

'So two nights ago you climbed up the wall and into his bathroom.'

'Yes. I knew what he usually did in the evening. I waited for him behind the bathroom door. When he came in, I killed him. Then I climbed back down and . . . well, you know what happened,' finished Ross.

Logan spoke to the three officers.

'You three, take Mr Ross to the police station. And when you get there, give him some different clothes and send those ones to the scientists. I think they'll find the material is the same as the material from Alex Maclennan's bathroom.'

Then she turned to Grant.

'Grant, you come with me.'

Chapter 8　*The last pieces*

When they got outside, Logan and Grant walked round to
Alice Maclennan's house in Polwarth Gardens.

Alice Maclennan opened the door.

'Well?' she asked in a quiet and rather sad voice.

'It was Ian Ross,' said Logan. 'Some officers are taking
him to the London Road Police Station right now.'

Alice Maclennan put her hand up to her mouth.

'Oh no! Ian,' she said. 'How terrible! Are you sure?'

'Yes. He's told us everything. Well, almost everything.'

Alice Maclennan looked at Logan strangely. 'Almost everything? What do you mean, Inspector?' she asked.

'Well, there's one thing he didn't tell us. He didn't tell us how long you and he were lovers. I was hoping you could tell us that.'

'Come in, Inspector,' said Alice Maclennan. 'Let's talk inside. It's warmer.'

They went into Alice Maclennan's living room and sat down.

'What I told you before was true. Alex and I were happily married until he started the restaurant,' began Alice Maclennan. 'I told you we had some problems then but . . . I couldn't tell you . . .' Alice Maclennan began to cry quietly.

'Go on,' said Logan softly.

'It started about eighteen months ago. Alex was spending all his time at the restaurant. I knew Ian was interested in me so I asked him round here one day when Alex was away.'

'And you became lovers,' said Logan.

'Yes. We were lovers for about a year.'

'Did your husband find out?'

'I don't know. I don't think so. At that time, Alex and I didn't talk very much. So I don't think he knew.'

'When did you and Ross stop seeing each other?' asked Logan.

'About six months ago,' said Alice Maclennan. 'I didn't want to spend any more time with Ian. And Alex was trying to make me happy again.'

'How did Ross feel about this?'

Alice Maclennan started to cry again.

Logan put her hand on Alice Maclennan's arm.

'Ian was terribly angry when I said we had to stop seeing each other,' said Alice Maclennan. She stopped and looked out of the window. Then she went on: 'I often asked myself why Ian and I were together. Did he really love me? Or did he love me because I was Alex's wife? When I left him, he said some terrible things.'

'He said he wanted you because you were Alex's?' asked Logan.

'Yes,' said Alice Maclennan quietly. 'I don't know if it was true. Perhaps he was just so angry that he said the first thing that came into his head. Perhaps it was half-true.' She stopped for a moment and then she asked: 'You don't think he killed Alex because I left him, do you?'

'No, I don't think so,' said Logan. 'Mainly I think he was angry that your husband was making so much money now. He asked for more money and your husband said no. I think the money was the most important thing for him.'

'I hope so, Inspector,' said Alice Maclennan. 'I really hope you're right.'

*   *   *

The next morning Grant and Logan sat in Logan's office. They were drinking coffee and talking about Ian Ross.

'Tell me, madam,' said Grant, 'how did you know it was Ross before you took off his hat?'

'It was a choice between Ross and Johnstone, but I always thought it was Ross,' said Logan. 'He was the only person who could climb up the wall. He was in the SAS. Climbing the wall was easy for him.'

'And what about Donald Johnstone?' asked Grant.

'Well, we had to see if it was him too,' said Logan. 'Just to be sure. But I never thought it was.'

Grant smiled.

'And how did you know that Ross and Alice Maclennan were lovers?'

'I only learnt that yesterday evening,' said Logan, 'from something that Ross said. He said he knew what Maclennan usually did at home in the evening. How did he know? I'm sure Maclennan didn't tell him what time he had a bath. And then I thought: "Perhaps Ross and Alice Maclennan were lovers. Perhaps they talked about Alex when they were together. Perhaps she told him." And I was right.'

Logan put her coffee cup down and looked at Grant.

'Anyway, you did very well last night, Sergeant,' she said. 'Where did you learn to take knives away from soldiers?'

'I've been in the police a long time, madam,' said Grant smiling. 'I've taken away one or two knives from people on Saturday nights.'

*   *   *

After Grant left, Logan made a phone call.

'Newsroom. Tam MacDonald speaking,' a voice said.

'Tam!' said Logan. 'It's Jenny Logan. You can buy me a drink this evening.'

'I'd love to, Jenny, my dear,' said Tam, 'but why?'

'Because you think I'm wonderful, and because I'm going to tell you who killed Alex Maclennan.'

'Tell me who killed Alex Maclennan, and I'll buy you dinner,' said Tam. 'And then I'll take you dancing at the best nightclub in town.'

Jenny laughed.

'I can think of better things to do than go dancing,' she said. 'Just meet me at Deacon Brodie's at seven o'clock.' And she smiled as she put the phone down.